I0487035

Quick Start with Project Management Fundamentals

Dr. Michael J. Williams

iUniverse, Inc.
New York   Bloomington

Quick Start with Project Management Fundamentals

Copyright © 2008 by Dr. Michael J. Williams

All rights reserved. No part of this book may be used or reproduced by any means, graphic, electronic, or mechanical, including photocopying, recording, taping or by any information storage retrieval system without the written permission of the publisher except in the case of brief quotations embodied in critical articles and reviews.

"PMI" and the PMI Logo are service and trademarks of the Project Management Institute, inc. Which are registered in the United States and other nations.

Limit of liability/Disclaimer of Warranty: While the publisher and author have used their best efforts in preparing this book, they make no representation or warranties with respect to the accuracy or completeness of the contents of this book and specifi cally disclaim any implied warranties of merchantability or fitness for a particular purpose. The advise and strategies contained herein may not be suitable for your project or for your situation.

iUniverse books may be ordered through booksellers or by contacting:

iUniverse
1663 Liberty Drive
Bloomington, IN 47403
www.iuniverse.com
1-800-Authors (1-800-288-4677)

Because of the dynamic nature of the Internet, any Web addresses or links contained in this book may have changed since publication and may no longer be valid. The views expressed in this work are solely those of the author and do not necessarily reflect the views of the publisher, and the publisher hereby disclaims any responsibility for them.

ISBN: 978-1-4401-0334-6 (pbk)
ISBN: 978-1-4401-0335-3 (ebk)

Printed in the United States of America
iUniverse rev. date: 12/10/2008

Table of Contents

ACKNOWLEDGMENTS

I would like to give special thanks to my wife Stephanie, for being so loving and patience during the research and writing of this book. I also want to thank my parents Thomas and Mae Williams for all the love and support they have given me through the years and also many other mentors that I have had from education, to business leaders. Men and women with true integrity. Thank you all. Most of all I want to thank God for giving me the abilities I have to be able to write this book, and give back to the world.

About the Author

Michael J. Williams is been in the IT field for 26 years and has been working in Project Management for over 13 years. Dr. Williams has spent most of his career working as a Consultant for several Fortune 500 companies, such as, Bell Labs, McGraw-Hill, Nationwide Insurance, Borden Companies,   NASA, Department of Defense, Applied Technology Resources and many others. Dr. Williams began working in Project Management in 1993 at which time he decided that project management was the way of the future. At that point he decided to direct his career in the direction of Project Management. Dr. Williams holds advanced degrees in Business and Law, and attended Villanova University to receive his IS/IT Project Management Professional Certification, and is currently managing multi-million dollar project for a fortune 100 company. Dr. Williams also wishes that a book such as this was available to him when he entered the project management field.

Forward

The Project management field is forever growing and expanding, and finding a book without all the technical in-depth jargon, for the beginner in Project Management does not seem to be out there. So I took it upon myself, for that very reason, to write a "Quick Start with Project Management" book. I wish a book like this existed when I was learning to be Project Manager. This book goes directly to the point without all the fluff of an 800 page Project Management book. You will, in time, need books like that as you grow in you knowledge base of Project Management. So I hope this book gives you the beginning insight you need to be successful as a Project Manager.

Chapter 1

What is Project Management ?

Definition of Project Management:

The definition of "Project Management", according to the 2004 "*PMBOK*" Guide Third Edition, Project Management is the application of knowledge, tools, and techniques to project activities to meet project requirements. Project Management is accomplished through the application and integration of the project management processes of initiating, planning, executing, monitoring and controlling, and closing the project.

From personnel experience, I found that know two projects are alike. Even when the projects seem to be basically the same, such as project requirements, equipment, and budgets. The Project Manager is, according to the 2004 "*PMBOK*" Guide Third Edition, is the person responsible for accomplishing the project objectives.

Managing a Project includes:
- Identifying Project Requirements
- Establishing clear and achievable objectives
- Balancing the competing demands for quality, scope, time, and cost Adapting the specification, plans, and approach to the different concerns and expectations of the various stakeholders.

Project Management has been around for thousands of years in one form or another. There had to be some form of Project Management when Egypt built the pyramids, when the Roman Empire built the coliseum, and when the Jewish people built the Temple in Jerusalem. All built over 1,500 years ago.

In business today Project Management has become so important and key to getting new products and services to market that Project Management processes and procedures have been developed to guide and assist all different types of businesses in accomplishing these goals. This book will lay the foundation and knowledge needed to accomplish the basic project management activities. This book covers:

- Defining a Project and Triple Constraint
- Project Charter
- Project Initiation
- Project Scope & Scope Management
- Project Estimating & Planning
- Project Risk Analysis & Management
- Project Time Management
- Project Execution
- Project Quality & Monitoring
- Project Closing & Lessoned Learned
- Project Methodologies

Project Management Terminology

Project Management today requires a consistent terminology that can be used across all projects. The following is a list of basic terms used in Project Management.

Acceptance testing

Applying performance and capability measurements to project deliverables to ensure that they meet specifications and requirements and satisfy the assignment and customer.

Activity

Element of work that is required by the project, use resources, and takes time and effort to complete. Activities have planned and expected durations, cost, and resource requirements, and are, in most cases, sub-divided into task requirements.

Acid Test
Most rigorous and severe form of testing for reliability, maintainability, and other criteria.

Acquisition
The ability to obtain supplies, servers, and resources for running a business, or completing a project.

Acquisition Control
A system or systems for acquiring project services, equipment, recourses, and material in a planned and an orderly managed process.

Backward Pass
A calculation of late finish and late start dates for uncompleted portions of all network activities. Determined by working backward through the network logic from the project's end date.

Baseline
The original plan (for a work package, activity, or project), plus or minus any approved changes. As the project progresses, you will use the baseline to measure against your project performance, i.e., schedule, cost, and scope.

Benchmark
A measured point of reference used to make comparisons at various completion points in a project.

Bottom-up-estimating
A cost or budget estimate derived by first estimating the cost of the project's elemental task at the lower levels of the WBS and then aggregating those estimates at successively higher levels of the WBS.

Breakdown

Identification of the smallest activities or task in a project for estimating, controlling, and monitoring purposes.

Break-even Point

A point in time during a project at which the value earned equals total cost.

Budget

A quantitative expression of the Project Management Plan to perform specific work. Used to present management's intentions and objectives to all levels of the organization, monitor implementation of the plans, and provided a quantitative basis for measuring and rewarding individual and unit performance.

Capability Maturity Model

A model used to describe the relative maturity of an organization, or subset of an organization, with respect to processes such as software engineering, people development, product development, systems integration, or project management, etc. The Capability Maturity Model consists of five maturity levels that have been described as end-state conditions. The current practice of an organization is compared to the model from which a determination is made as to which of the five levels of the organization's practices represent. This information is then used to guide the organization into establishing action plans to advance to the next level.

CCB – Change Control Board

A formally constituted group of stakeholders responsible for approving or rejecting changes to a project baseline.

Change Control

1.) The process of monitoring and dealing with changes to the schedule, cost, or scope of a project, or its overall objectives. 2.) Defined processes and procedures for "Change Management" during the "Project Life Cycle (PLC).

Change Management

A process used to make changes to a project already in progress, i.e., a "Change Management Systems".

Change Management Plan

1.) A predetermined document approach to implementing configuration controls. 2.) Approach used to assimilate a new system or set of procedures in a project.

Change Request

1.) A request or modification to the terms of a contract or to the description of the product or services to be provided. 2.) A formal written statement requesting to make a change or modification to a deliverable.

Closeout Phase

The fifth phase in the project life cycle where all outstanding deliverables are completed and documented in preparation for releasing the product or service over to the customer.

Communication

Effective transfer of information from one party to another. Communications comprises of four elements: 1.) Communicator or sender of message. 2.) Message 3.) Medium of the message. 4.) Receiver of the message.

Communication Channel

A means of communication used to transmit a message. Three types of communication channels exist in the project management environment. 1.) Formal Communication – Communication within the companies formal communication structure used to transmit goals, policies, and directives. 2.) Informal Communication – Communication outside the companies formal communication structure. 3.) Unofficial Communication – Interpersonal communication within the companies social structure.

Conflict Management

The process by which individuals use managerial techniques to deal with disagreements, both personal and technical while working on a project.

Constraint

1.) A restriction that affects the scope of the project. 2.) Any factor that affects when and how an activity or task can be scheduled. 3.) Any factor that limits the project team's performance and options.

Contingency Plan

A plan that identifies alternative plan or strategy to be used if specified risk come forward and occur.

Cost Estimating

The process used to estimate the cost of the resources needed to perform and complete the project. Includes an economic evaluation, an assessment of project investment cost, and a forecast of future trends and costs.

Cost Management

A function required to maintain effective financial controls of the project by evaluating, estimating, budgeting, monitoring, analyzing, forecasting, and reporting cost information.

Cost Management Plan

A document that describes how cost will be managed by the project manager and the project team.

Crashing

Crashing is the term used when taking action to decease the total project duration by adding additional resources such as, human and material, to the project schedule without altering the sequence of activities or tasks. The objective of crashing is to obtain the maximum compression duration for the least cost.

Critical Path

A critical path in a project network diagram is the path that determines the earliest completion date of the project. The critical path will change if task that are on the critical path completed other than on the completion date.

Customer Acceptance

A document that is signed off by the customer that all project deliverables have satisfied all customer requirements.

Critical Path Method (CPM)

Network analysis technique used to predict project duration by analyzing the sequence of activities (path) that has the least amount of scheduling flexibility (the least amount of float). Early dates are calculated by a forward pass using a specified start date. Late dates are calculated by a backward pass starting from a specified completion date (usually the forward pass's calculated early finish date for the project.

Critical Path Network (CPN)

Project plan consisting of activities and their logical relationships to one another. This the output of the critical path method.

Decision Theory

Technique used in risk quantification to assist in decision making, which points to the best possible course of action, considering project uncertainties.

Decision Tree

Diagram that shows key interactions among decisions and associated chance events as they are understood by the decision maker. Branches of the tree represent either decisions or chance events. The decision tree diagram provides for the consideration of the probability of each outcome.

Delegation

The process of distributing authority from the project manager to another individual working on the project.

Deliverable

A measurable, tangible, verifiable outcome, result, or item that must be produced to complete a project or part of a project. Often used more narrowly in reference to an external deliverable, which is a deliverable that is subject to approval by the project sponsor or stakeholder.

Delphi Technique

Form of participative expert judgment; an iterative, anonymous, interactive technique using survey methods to derive consensus on work estimates, approaches, and issues.

Dependency

Logical relationship between and among tasks of a project's WBS, which can be graphically depicted on a network diagram.

Design

Creation of the description of a product or service, in the form of specifications, drawings, data flow diagrams, or any other methods, to provide detailed information on how to build the product or perform the service.

Development Methodology

Set of mutually supportive and integrated processes and procedures organized into a series of phases constituting the development cycle of a product or service.

Deviation

(A) Departure from established requirements. (B) Written authorization, granted before proceeding with departure from a specific design or requirement.

Duration (DU)

The number of work periods required to complete an activity or other project elements. Usually expressed as hours, workdays, or workweeks. It is sometimes incorrectly equated with elapsed time.

Effort

Number of labor units required to complete an activity or other project element. May be expressed as staff hours, days, or weeks. Should not be confused with duration.

Elapsed Time

Conventional concept of time with a 60 minute hour and a 365 day year. Accounts for all time, not just time spent on the project.

End Product

The end product / deliverable resulting from the project.

End User

A Person or group for whom all project's service's or product's developed for.

Engineering Change Order or Change Order Process

A directive to make a change / improvement, after the initial design has been approved by management, to the service or product design.

Escalation

Conversion of past to present prices or present to future prices through use of a price index.

Estimate

The assessment of likely quantitative result, usually applied to project cost and durations.

Estimate at Completion (EAC)

The expected total cost of an activity, group of activities, or total project when the work is complete.

Estimated Cost

Anticipated cost of performance of a project from start to finish.

Estimating

Forecasting the cost, schedule, and resource requirements needed to produce a specific deliverable.

Event

(1) Activity that doers not use a resource; a milestone. (2) End state for one or more activities that occur at a specific point in time. (3) A significant event or occurrence that obligates the company to take a specific action at a given point in time. (4) A key component of risk. It is usually a description of the a negative or a positive event associated with risk.

Event-on-Node

Used in Network diagramming. A technique in which events are represented by boxes (or nodes) connected by arrows to show the sequence in which the events are to occur.

Exception Report

A document that includes only significant variance from the project baseline.

Executed Process

Activities associated with coordinating people and other resources to implement the project plan.

Execution Phase

(See Implementation Phase)

Expert Authority

A person that holds knowledge or expertise in a given area.

External Risk

A risk that is outside or beyond the control or influence of the project, or the project team.

Fast Tracking

It is the process of compressing the project schedule by overlapping activities normally performed in sequence, such as the design and testing phase in a project.

Fault Tolerance

A method used to make a computer or network system resistant to software errors and hardware malfunctions.

Feasibility

The assessment of the capability for successful implementation of a project. Also the probability and suitability of accomplishment.

Feasibility Study

The economic potential and the practicality of a project meeting a need within the company.

Finish Date

Point in time associated with an activity's or project's completion. Usually qualified by terms such as actual, planned, estimated agreements, or leases.

Finish-to-Finish (FF)

A relationship in a precedence diagramming method network in which one activity must end before the successor activity can end.

Finish-to-Start (FS)

A relationship in a precedence diagramming method network in which one activity must end before the successor activity can start.

Float

The Amount of time that an activity may be delayed from its early start date without delaying the entire project end date.

Floating Task

Task that can be performed earlier or later in the schedule without affecting the project duration or critical path.

Flow Diagram

A graphic representation of work flow and the logical sequence of the work elements without regard to a time scale. Used to show the logic associated with a process rather than a duration for completion of work.

Flow Chart

A diagram consisting of symbols depicting a physical process, a thought process, or an algorithm. Shows how the various elements of a system or process relate and which can be used for continues process improvement.

Forward Scheduling

A method in which the project start date is fixed and task duration and dependency information is used to compute the corresponding project completion date.

Free Float

Amount of time that an activity may be delayed without delaying the early start of any immediately succeeding activities.

Functional Baseline

Initial approved functional configuration identification.

Functional Breakdown Structure (FBS)

Hierarchical structure relating the function of a product or service. Used in value analysis techniques.

Gantt Chart

It is graphic display of schedule-related information. Generally, activities or other project elements are listed down the left side of the chart, dates are shown across the top, and activity duration are displayed against the "x" and "y" axes as date-placed horizontal bars. Named after its creator Henry Gantt.

Go/No-Go

(1) The major decision point in the project life cycle. (2) Measure that allows a manager to decide whether to continue, change, or end an activity or project. (3) Type of gauge that tells an inspector if an object's dimension is within certain limits.

Histogram

A timeline chart that shows the use of a resource over time.

Holistic View

Is oriented toward viewing the whole rather than considering each piece individually.

Implementation Phase

Third of four sequential phases in the project life cycle in which the project plan is executed, monitored, and controlled. Also called the execution or operation phase.

Initial Project Plan

(1) Top-down, high level plan used to document the early approach to a project; usually contains resource manager commitments and a preliminary technical solution. (2) Method for communication during the delegation of the project responsibility and acceptance of the project commitments.

Initiation Process

The procedures for recognizing that a project or phase should begin and committing to start the project.

Initiation

The process of formally recognizing that a new project exists or that an existing project should continue into its next phase.

Just in Time

Approach used to manage resources, requirements, and production so that the right material arrives at the right place at the right time, just in time for use.

Kick-Off Meeting

A meeting held to acquaint stakeholders and staff with the project and each other. It's the starting point of a project.

Lag

The modification of a logical relationship in a schedule such that there is a delay in the successor task.

Late Finish Date (LF)

The latest possible point in time that an activity may end without a delay in the project finish date. Used in the critical path method.

Late Start Date (LS)

The latest possible point in time that an activity may begin without delaying the project finish date. Used in the critical path method.

Lead

The modification of a logical relationship in a schedule such that there is an acceleration of the successor task. For example, in a finish-to-start dependency with a 5-day lead, the successor activity can start 5 days before the predecessor has finished. *See* also lag.

Lead Time

The time required to wait for a product, service, material, or resources, after ordering or making a request for such things.

Leader

The individual who uses his or her influence in a group to motivate others to do something for the organization, project etc.

Life Cycle

The entire useful life of a product or service, usually divided into sequential phases, which include initiation, development, execution, operation, maintenance, and disposal or termination.

Loaded Rates

The charges for human and material resources that incorporate both hourly or per-use charges and all additional general and administrative cost associated with their use.

Loop

The network path that passes the same node twice. Loops cannot be analyzed using network analysis techniques such as CPM and PERT but are allowed in GERT.

Make or Buy Analysis

The management technique used to determine whether a particular product or service can be produced or performed cost effectively by the performing company or should be contracted out to another company to build the product or perform the service.

Management Plan

The document or documents that describes the overall guidelines under which the project is organized, administered, and managed to ensure timely accomplishment of the project objectives.

Mandatory Dependency

The dependency inherent in the nature of the work being done, such as physical limitations.

Master Schedule

Is the primary schedule used to baseline and drive the entire project.

Material Requirement Planning (MRP)

The planning and material ordering technique based on the known or forecast final demand requirements for each item, lead time for each fabricated or purchased item, and existing inventories of all items and types.

Matrix Organization

The project organization structure in which the project manager shares responsibility with the functional manager to assign priorities and direct the work of individuals assigned to the project.

Maturity Level

A defined position in an achievement scale that establishes the attainment of certain capabilities.

Milestone

(1) An event with zero duration and requiring no resources. Used to measure the progress of a project and signifies completion or start of a major deliverable or other significant metric such as cost incurred, hours used, payment made, etc. (2) Identifiable point in a project or set of activities that represent a reporting requirement or completion of a large or important set of activities.

Mission Statement

The description prepared and endorsed by members of the company or team that answers these questions: (1) What do we do ? (2) For whom do we do it for ? (3) How do we go about it ? (4) Used as the guide for making decisions in the project.

Mitigation

Risk response strategy that decrease risk by lowering the probability of a risk event's occurrence or reducing the effect of the risk should it occur.

Monitor

Acquire and analyze data on an ongoing basis so that action can be taken when progress fails to match plans and meet objectives.

Monte Carlo Analysis

Schedule or cost risk assessment technique that entails performing a project simulation many times to calculate a likely distribution of results.

Negative Float

A situation in which the difference between the late (start or finish) date and early (start or finish) date of an activity is a negative number.

Net Present Value (NPV)

A financial calculation that takes into account the time values of a stream of income and expenditures at a given interest rate.

Network

(1) Graphic depiction of the relationship of projects work (activities and task). (2) Communication facility that connects end systems.

Network Diagram

Schematic display of the logical relationships of project activities, usually drawn from left to right to reflect project chronology.

Network Path

A continuous series of connected activities in a project network diagram.

Node

Junction point joined to some or all of the other dependency lines in a network; an intersection of two or more lines or arrows.

Objective

(1) End toward which effort is directed; a predetermined result. (2) Organizational performance criteria to be achieved and measured in the use of organizational resources.

Organization Chart

A graphic display of reporting relationship that provides a general framework of the organization.

Organizational Breakdown Structure (OBS)

A toll used to show the work units or work packages that are assigned to specific organizational units.

Parallel Tasks

An independent task that proceed concurrently.

Pareto Diagram

Histogram, ordered by frequency of occurrence that shows the number of results that were generated by each identified cause.

Pareto's Law

The principle, espoused by Joseph Juran and based on the work of the nineteenth century Italian economist Vilfredo Pareto, starting that a relatively small number of cause typically will produce a large majority of problems or defects. Improvement efforts are usually most cost-effective when focused on a few high impact causes.

Peer Review

The review of a project or phase of a project by individuals with equivalent knowledge and background who are not currently members of the project team and have not participated in the development of the project.

Performance Measurement Baseline

A time-based budget plan used to measure performance. Formed by the budgets assigned to scheduled cost accounts and the applicable indirect budgets.

Performance Review

A meeting held periodically to access project status or progress.

PERT

Performance Evaluation and Review Technique

PERT Chart

Specific type of project network diagram.

Phase Exit or Phase Gate or Control Gate

A specific point in time during the project life cycle at which key project stakeholders convene to assess performance to date, validate key project assumptions, analyze current and future market conditions, and discuss other factors to determine whether the project should: (1) Be terminated, (2) Proceed according to the original plan, (3) Proceed based on a revised plan.

Phased Planning

An approach used to plan only to the level of detail that is known at the time.

Pilot

A trial apparatus or operation used to validate a proposed solution in a live environment.

PM

Stands for: Project Management

PMBOK

Stands for: Project Management Body of Knowledge

PMI

Stands for: Project Management Institute

PMO

Stands for: Project Management Office

PMP

Stands for: Project Management Professional

Precedence Diagramming Method (PDM)

A network diagramming technique in which activities are represented by boxes (or nodes) and linked by precedence relationship lines to show the sequence in which the activities are to be performed. The nodes are connected with arrows to show the dependencies. Four types of relationships are possible: Finish-to-finish, Finish-to-start, Start-to -finish, and start-to-start. Also called activity-on-node (AON).

Program Evaluation and Review Technique (PERT)

An event oriented, probability based network analysis technique used to estimate project duration when there is a high degree of uncertainty with the individual activity duration estimate. PERT applies the critical path method to a weighted average duration estimate. The formula is: <u>O + 4 (ML) + p</u>6 Where O = optimistic time, ML = most likely time, and P = pessimistic time.

Program Management

Management of a related series of project over a period of time, to accomplish broad goals to which the individual projects contribute.

Project

Temporary undertaking to create a unique product or service with a defined start and end point and specific objective that, when attained, signify completion.

Project Baseline

Project Management frame of reference established based on the detailed project plan and incorporating the project's cost, schedule, and quality objectives to serve as the basis for measuring progress, comparing planned and actual events and expenditures, and identifying and executing changes to the project's scope of work.

Project Business Case

A document containing the analysis and results of the business assessments providing the justification to pursue a project opportunity.

Project Charter

A document issued by senior management that gives the project manager authority to apply company resources to the project activities and formally recognizes the existence of a project.

Project Closeout

A process to provide for the project acceptance by the project sponsor, completion of various project records, and final closing/ending of the project.

Project Definition

A name used to identify any number of tools or templates that capture important project information to ensure that the project team address, and agrees upon, key project terms and elements.

Project Duration

The length of time a project last from start date to finish date.

Project Execution

Third of four sequential phases in the project life cycle in which the project plan is executed, monitored, and controlled. Also called the execution or operation phase.

Project Finish Date

The latest calendar finish date of all activities on the project, based on network or resource allocation process calculations.

Project Initiation

The process of formally recognizing that a new project exists or that an existing project should continue into its next phase.

Project Integration Management

Part of project management that includes the processes required to ensure that the various project elements are coordinated effectively. Consists of project plan development, project plan execution, and overall changes control

Project Life Cycle

A collection of generally sequential project phases whose specific name and number are determined by the company or organization involved in the project. Generally includes the major steps involved in conceptualizing, designing, developing, and putting into operation the project's technical performance deliverables.

Project Management (PM)

The application of knowledge, skills, tools, and techniques to project activities to meet or exceed stakeholder needs and expectations from a project.

Project Management Body of Knowledge (PMBOK)

The totality of knowledge within the project management profession.

Project Management Controls

The processes and procedures designed to ensure that project performance information is collected, analyzed, and reviewed by appropriate stakeholders and used to decide any course of action to achieve the project's objectives.

Project Management Institute (PMI), Inc.

The international, nonprofit professional association dedicated to advancing The discipline of project management and state-of-the-art project management practices.

Project Management Methodology

A highly detailed description of the procedures to be followed in a project life cycle. Often includes forms, charts, checklists, and templates to ensure structure and consistency.

Project Management Professional (PMP)

The professional certification awarded by the Project Management Institute to individuals who have met the required knowledge, education, and experience in the discipline of project management.

Project Management Software

There is special software that has been developed to aid Project Managers in planning and executing there projects.

Project Manager

The person that is responsible for managing the overall project and its deliverables from start to finish.

Project Metrics

This is a measurable criteria that indicates the overall status or performance of a project, program, or project management practice.

Project Network Diagram

A graphical depiction of the logical relationships between and among project activities.

Project Management Office (PMO)

(1) An organizational office established to assist project managers Throughout the organization in implementing project management Principles, practices, methodologies, tools, and techniques. (2) An organizational entity established to complete a specific project or Series of projects, usually headed by a project manager.

Project Phase

A collection of logically related project activities, usually resulting in the completion of a major deliverable. Collectively, the project phases compose the project life cycle.

Project Plan

The formal, approved document, in summarized or detailed form, used to guide both project execution and control of the overall project.

Project Plan Execution

The process of executing the project through the various project phases.

Project Portfolio

A collection of various projects to be managed concurrently. Also call portfolio management.

Project Reporting

During the project the project manager and the project team will need to communicate information about the project status and progress. This is called project reporting.

Project Risk

The cumulative effect of the probability of uncertain occurrences that may affect the project in either a positive or negative way. Also the degree of exposure to negative events and their probable consequences.

Project Risk Management

This is the part of Project Management that includes the processes involved with identifying, analyzing, and responding to project risk. This consists of risk identification, risk quantification, risk response development, and risk response control.

Project Schedule

The planned dates laid out to perform activities and meet milestones on the project schedule.

Project Scope

This is all the work required to deliver a project's product or service with the specific features and functions required to complete the project.

Project Scope Management

The part of project management that includes the processes required to ensure that the project includes all the work required, and only the work required, to successfully complete the project. This consists of project initiation, scope planning, scope definition, scope verification, and scope change control.

Project Segments

The subdivisions of the project expressed as manageable and workable project components.

Project Sponsor

The person or persons in an organization whose support and approval is required for a project to start and be able to continue.

Project Strategy

It is the plan with policies to provide general direction of how resources will be used to accomplish project goals and objectives.

Project Team

It is the group of people with complementary skills, with a common purpose, shared goals, and mutual accountability who share responsibility for accomplishing project goals and who report either full or part time to the project manager.

Project Time Management

The part of project management that include the processes required to ensure that the project is completed on time. This consist of activity definition, activity sequencing, activity duration estimating, schedule development, and schedule control.

Project WBS

Project Work Breakdown Structure.

Projection

It is the estimate of future performance based on the review of historical information, present situation, and future outlook.

Proof of Concept

The evidence to support acceptance of a proposed solution or solutions.

Proposal

The offer submitted by a contractor to enter into a contract, contract modification or termination settlement.

Punch List

The list prepared when the project is almost completed to show the items of work remaining to fulfill the projects scope.

Punitive Damages

The monetary compensation, over and above the actual damages, sought by a plaintiff to punish a seller for nonperformance or other wrongful acts performed by defendant.

Purchase Order

This is and offer to buy certain supplies, services, or construction from sources based on specified terms and conditions.

QA

(Quality Assurance) The process of regularly evaluating overall project performance to provide confidence that the project will satisfy relevant quality standards.

QC

(Quality Control) The monitoring of specific project results to determine whether they comply with relevant quality standards and identification of ways to eliminate causes of unsatisfactory performance.

Quality Gate

The predefined completion criterion for a task, including audits, walk- through, and inspections that provide an assessments of progress, processes used, and project products to be delivered.

Qualitative Risk Assessment

The non-numeric description of a risk, including the likelihood that it will occur, its impact, the methods for containing the impact, possible fallback or recovery measures, and ownership data.

Quality Loop

Conceptual model of interacting activities that influence the quality of a product or service in various stages ranging from needs identification to assessment of whether the needs have been satisfied.

Quality Management

The planning, organizing, staffing, coordinating, directing, and controlling activities of management with the objective of achieving the required quality.

Quality Process Review

The technical process of using data to determine how the actual project results compare with the quality specification or requirements.

Quantitative Risk Assessment

The numeric analysis of risk estimates including probability of occurrence to forecast the project's schedule and cost using probabilistic data and other identified uncertainties to determine likely outcomes.

Recovery Schedule

A special schedule showing efforts to take to recover time lost on the project as compared to the master schedule.

Reference Base

The source of detailed cost information within a function or organization from which estimates and budgets may, in part, be established for work relating to the function.

Regression Analysis

The statistical technique used to establish and graphically depict the relationship of a dependent variable to one or more independent variables.

Request for Proposal (RFP)

A type of bid document used to solicit proposals from prospective contractors for any product or service. Mainly used when items or services are of complex nature and assumes that negotiation will take place between the buyer and the contractor.

Request for Quotation (RFQ)

This is usually a price quote. Similar to a RFP but generally with lower monetary amount involved in the quote process.

Requirements Analysis

The process of evaluating the customer's stated needs and validating them against specific organizational requirements and plans.

Resource Allocation

The process of assigning resources to the given project, or the activities in a network while recognizing any resource constraints and requirements; adjusting activity level start and finish dates to conform to resource availability and use.

Resource Breakdown Structure (RSB)

This is a variation of the organizational breakdown structure used to show which work elements are assigned to individuals.

Review Board or Change Review Board

A committee of senior personnel for reviewing and approving changes to a project or service being created.

Resource Leveling

(1) Practicing a form of network analysis in which scheduling decisions (start and finish dates) are driven by resource management issue (such as limited resource availability or changes in resource levels). (2) Evening out the peaks and valleys of resource requirements so that a fixed amount of resources can be used over time. (3) Ensuring that a resource is maximized but not used beyond its limits.

Resource Loading

One of the project manager's major tasks is designating the amount and type of resources to be assigned to a specific activity in a certain period.

Resource Matrix

A structure used to allocate types of resources to tasks by listing the tasks in the WBS along the vertical axis and the resources required along the horizontal axis.

Resource Plan

A document used to describe the number of resources needed to accomplish the project work and the steps necessary to obtain resources.

Resource Requirements

The output of the resource planning process, which describes the types and quantities of resources required for each element of the WBS. Resources are then obtained through staff acquisition or procurement.

Resource Planning

The process of formulating project risk management strategies, including allocating responsibility to the project's various functional areas. May involve avoidance, acceptance, mitigation, and the use of the certain tools and techniques such as deflection and contingency planning.

Risk Analysis

Analysis of the probability that certain undesirable and beneficial events will occur and their impact on attaining project objectives.

Risk Assessment

(1) The review, examination, and judgment to see whether the identified risks are acceptable according to proposed actions. (2) It's the identification and quantification of project risks to ensure that they are understood and can be prioritized. Also called risk evaluation.

Risk Event Status

(1) It's the measure of importance of a risk event. (2) Its the probability and impact of a risk as of the data date.

Risk Exposure

(1) Its the impact value of a risk multiplied by its probability of occurring. (2) Loss provision made for a risk; requires that a sufficient number of situations in which risk could occur have been analyzed.

Risk Management Plan

It is the documentation of the procedures to be used to manage risk during the life of a project and the parties responsible for managing various areas of risk.

Schedule

The time sequenced plan of activities or task used to direct and control project execution. Usually shown in milestones on a Gantt, or other bar chart.

Schedule Baseline

A approved project schedule that serve as the basis for measuring and reporting schedule performance.

Scope

Sum of the products and services to be provided by the project.

Scope change

The modification to the agreed-upon project scope as defined by the approved WBS.

Scope Creep

The gradual progressive increase of the project's scope such that it is not noticed by the project management team or the customer. This is when additional products or services are added to the project with out official change management approval process.

Six Sigma

Quality concept and aim developed by Motorola, Inc. and defined as a measure of goodness-the capability of a process to produce perfect work. Six sigma refers to the number of standard deviations from the average setting of a process to the tolerance limit, which in statistical terms translates to 3.4 defects per million opportunities for error.

Slack

See Float

SOW

Stands for "Statement of Work" This is the work to be performed on a project.

Sponsor

The individual or group in the performing organization providing the financial resources, in cash or in kind, for the project.

Stage Gate

See Control Gate

Stakeholder

A individual or organization who is actively involved in the project or whose interest may be affected, either positively or negatively as a result of the project execution or successful project completion.

Start-to-finish

The relationship in the precedence diagramming method network in which one activity must start before the successor activity can finish.

Start-to-start

The relationship in the precedence diagramming method network in which one activity must start before successor activity can start.

Strategic Planning

Type of planning to establish the mission, objective, goals, and strategies of the company's future state.

SWOT

Strengths-weaknesses-opportunities-threats analysis.

Task

The well defined component of project work. The task assigned to complete a project, or and allotment of work.

Template

A set of guidelines that provides sample outlines, forms, checklists, and other documents.

Top down estimating

The cost estimating that begins with the top level of the WBS and then works down to successively lower levels.

Trend Analysis

(1) The use of mathematical techniques to forecast future outcomes based on historical results. (2) The examination of project results over time to determine whether performance is improving or deteriorating.

Triple Constraint

The term used to identify what is generally regarded as the three most important factors that a project manager needs to consider in any project: time, cost, and scope (specifications).

Typically represent as a triangle, each of these constraints, when changed, will impact one or both of the others. They do not exist in isolation in any project.

Work Breakdown Structure (WBS)

A hierarchically-structured grouping of project elements that organizes and defines the total scope of the project. Each descending level is an increasingly detailed definition of a project component. Project components may be products (a product-oriented WBS) or tasks (a task oriented WBS).

WBS Dictionary

A collection of work packages descriptions that includes, among others, planning information such as schedule dates, cost budgets, and staff assignments.

Work Acceptance

The work that is considered accepted when it is conducted, documented, and verified according to acceptance criteria provided in the technical specifications and contract documents.

Work Package

It is a deliverable at the lowest level of the WBS. May be divided into several activities and used to identify and control work flows in the organization.

Work Unit

It is a calendar time unit when work may be performed on an activity or activities on a project.

NOTES:

_____

_____

_____

_____

_____

_____

_____

_____

_____

_____

_____

_____

_____

_____

_____

_____

_____

_____

Chapter 2

Project Management Institute (PMI)

Defining a Project and the Triple Constraint

The Project Management Institute (PMI)

PMI is an international professional society for project managers, and this this professional society was found in 1969. The PMI has continued to attract professional members last reporting more than 133,000 members worldwide in May 2004. A good percentage of the PMI member are in the Information Technology field. PMI has created many different groups called, Specific Interest Groups (SIG's) that enable members, in different fields, to share specific information about their profession with others in different fields of expertise.

Project Management Certification (PMP)

The Project Management Institute has a certification call the Project Management Professional Certification (PMP). This certification is obtain through documented experience, has agreed to follow the PMI code, and has demonstrated knowledge of the PMP field, by taking and passing a comprehensive examination provide by the Project Management Institute. The number of people earning their PMP certifications is growing at and increasing rate. In the early 1990's there was only about 1,000 members certified in this field. By the mid 1990's their was nearly 81,000 certified Project Management Professional worldwide.

Project Management Ethics

When viewing the subject of ethics, you need look at the profession as a whole. Ethics is a very important part of any and all professions. Project Management is no different. Project Managers often are faced with ethical dilemmas in their day-today dealings with sponsors, stakeholders, management, and subordinates. If it does not feel right it most likely isn't.

What a Project is or is Not

Let's start with defining what a project is and is not. All projects have a definite start and end date. If whatever you are working on is performed in the normal operation of running the business this not a project and this is the key different between a project and normal business activities. A project is a temporary undertaking to create a specific product or service. Starting and Information Technology project involves the use of software, hardware and people. Most projects are unique to there environment, temporary, and developed incrementally. All projects require resources, have a sponsor/stakeholder, and involve varying levels of uncertainty.

Triple Constraint

Each and every project is constrained in one or more different ways by its scope, time, and cost goals. Within project management these limitation are called the "Triple Constraint". For a project to be successful, the project manager must balance the cost, scope, and time in a project. When executing a project, the following must be considered: Time – How long it will take to complete a project. This is driven by the project schedule. Scope – The work to be performed in the project. This evolves what products or services, and what results the sponsor or stakeholder expects from the project. Cost– What will the cost be to complete the project? This includes all resources such as personnel, computers, etc. This is what is defined as the project budget.

The managing of the Triple Constraint involves the tradeoffs between time, scope, cost projections and goals for the project. There are times when you may need to increase the cost in a project to add more personnel to complete the project on time and in scope. The following is a diagram of the "Triple Constraint" Figure 2.1.

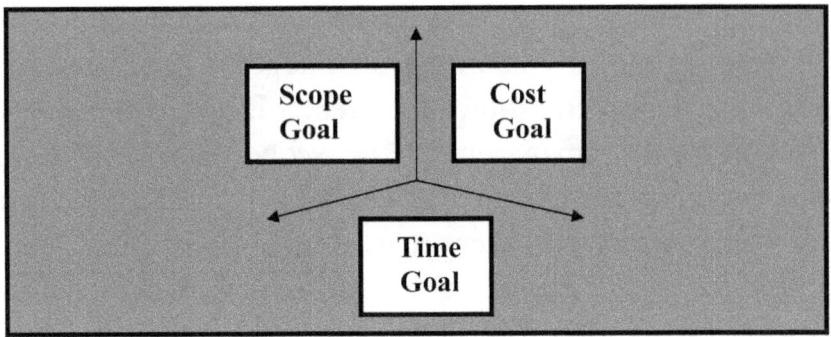

Figure 2.1

The main point of the triple constraint is to use these guiding principle to successfully manage and complete a project meeting all three goals, Time, Scope, and Cost.

<u>Project Stakeholders</u>

In any project there is a person or a group of people call Stakeholder or stakeholders. Stakeholders are the people that are involved in or affected by project activities and include the project team, support staff, any customers, end users, suppliers, opponents, and most of all the project sponsor.

As you can see, stakeholders come in many different forms, and each form has different expectation and deliverables from the project being developed by the project team. The project manager, and the project team, must keep these differences in mind during the project. Most of the differences should be identified when the "Business Case Analysis" is performed, and before the project is even initiated.

9 Project Management Knowledge Areas

The "Project Management Knowledge Areas" are used by the project manager and the team for completing a project on time, in scope, and in within budget. There are nine project management knowledge areas. The core knowledge areas of project management are scope, time, cost, and quality management. You may wonder why these are the core knowledge areas, well, they are used by project management to lead to specific project objectives. The following is a brief description of each core knowledge areas: Project Scope Management – It involves the defining and managing of all the work that is required to complete any project successfully. Project Time Management – This includes estimating the time it will take to complete the work, developing an acceptable project schedule, and ensuring timely completion of all project deliverables. Project Cost Management – This is the process used to prepare and manage the budget for the project. Project Quality Management – This is the process used for ensuring that the project is able to satisfy the stated objective by the project charter for which the project was undertaken. There are four facilitating knowledge areas in project management. They are, human resources, communications, risk, and procurement management. These are called facilitating areas because they are processes that are used to achieve the project objectives. The following is a brief description of each facilitating knowledge areas: Project Human Resources Management – The project Manager is concerned with making the most effective use of the personnel that are involved with all aspects of the project. Project Communications Management – This is a very key and Important part of project management. It involves generating, collecting, disseminating, distributing, and storing all the projects information. Including lessons learn at the end of the project. Project Risk Management – We use Risk Management to identify potential hazards to a project. By identifying, analyzing, and responding to any and all risk the will be related to the project, the project manager, and the project team can take steps to mitigate the risk. Project Procurement Management – This normally involves procuring goods and services, from one or more sources outside the company.

NOTES:

_____

_____

_____

_____

_____

_____

_____

_____

_____

_____

_____

_____

_____

_____

_____

_____

Chapter 3

Project Initiation
Starting a Project

What is Project Initiation?

It is just what it sounds like. It is the process of beginning a project. From a project management perspective, initiating a project includes, recognizing and starting the first phase of the project. Organizations really need to put a considerable amount of thought into what projects they will undertake, and for what reasons. This insures that the organization initiates the right kind of projects. The selection of projects for initiation, therefore, is crucial, as is the selection of the right project manager. When selecting the right project, you will need to take several things into account. The following is a list of things to consider when initiating a project: Does this project fit the company or organization? Does the company or organization have the infrastructure to perform / support a project like this? Does the company or organization have the personnel inside or will they need to contract outside to retain the talent they need? Does the company or organization have all the other resources needed to accomplish the project, or will they need to go outside to gain these resources?

What do you manage on a Project?

These are the three most important things to remember to manage on a project. We covered these three topics back in chapter 2, but will cover them again here with some additional information.

- Scope
- Cost   **The Triple Constraint**
- Time

We seek to maximize scope with out allowing scope creep. we will cover scope creep later, while keeping cost down, and deliverables on time. One of the key things also to keep in mind when working a project is to keep the utmost quality in mind. You could keep scope, cost, and time under control, but if you deliver a poor product or service to the customer, you may have not taken on the project at all.

The who's who on a Project

On a project there are many different players, and they perform different roles. One person can perform many different roles, while another individual my only perform one. So now lets examine the different roles that the players perform on a project.

Project Manager

If you are the project manager on a project, you have and exciting job ahead of you, if you work for a well run company or organization. If not, you may feel as if you have had the curse of the pharaoh put upon you. The project manager is responsible for the following: In many cases, defining the product or service being provided to the customer. This includes, both features and its specifications, and its value to the company or organization. Defining and writing the project plan. This encompasses how the project will be completed. Creating the project team, and laying out there job assignments, and leading the team to success. A key responsibility is to keep track of everything, catching problems as early as possible, and providing the needed corrective actions to keep the project moving forward to completion. Managing all deliverables and the delivery process, ensuring that the customer is satisfied with the final product or service.

Project Sponsor

Is the individual, usually a senior executive, or a group that is responsible for bringing the project into existence. The sponsor has the authority over both customer and the project team as a whole. The sponsor is the one that will kick off the project at the initial meeting, it is also their job to promote the project to the highest levels of the company or organization.

Project Lead

This is the senior individual in the customer organization or department. The primary responsibility of the project lead is to define all the requirements or make sure that the members of the customers team work with the project team. This sometimes can be a very daunting task. The project lead also has the responsibility for having the customer learn and test the new product or service. They can also participate in defining the project's final results.

Project Team

The project team, led by the project manager, carry's out the daily task that are required to complete the project. This can be architects, programmers, Analyst, Engineers etc.

Customer

Believe it or not, the customer is just not a single person, although it can be a single person in some cases. The customer is everyone in the receiving and using the results of the project.

Stakeholder

In most cases, a stakeholder is anyone the may be effected by the project.

Vendors and Consultants

Vendors, in most cases, are providing some kind of hardware, Software or application that either will be used to run the project, like MS Project, or used by the company, and the application developers on the project team will make modification to. Vendors also provide consulting services to companies or organizations for their expertise in a given subject matter area. Consultants are used quite often on project because they bring expertise that the company does not have internally.

Project Charter

The project charter is a document that lays out what will be accomplished during the project. The dictionary definition is: A document issued by senior management that gives the project manager authority to apply company resources to the project activities and formally recognizes the existence of a project. In many cases additional information is included in the project charter. Such as: The purpose of the project. What the project will be performing for the company. What the project will not be performing for the company. What the benefits of the project will be for the company. What resources will be made available for the project. The time frame to build the product or service. Besides using a Project Charter, some companies just use a simple letter of agreement as the go ahead for the project. The project charter is a key output of the project initiation process.

Next we will go into writing the project scope statement, and start the Project Management Process.

NOTES:

_____

_____

_____

_____

_____

_____

_____

_____

_____

_____

_____

_____

_____

_____

_____

_____

_____

Chapter 4

Project Scope
&
Scope Management

What is Project Scope Management?

One of the key factors in project management, and one of the most difficult aspects of project management, is defining the scope of a project. The scope of a project refers to "all" the work involved in putting together the products of the project and the processes used to create them.

Project scope management includes all the processes involved in defining and controlling what will or will not be included in a particular project. This ensures that the stakeholders and the project team have a clear understanding on what will be produced, the time to produces it, the resources that will be used and the processes the project team will use to produce them.

Five main processes areas have been identified in project scope Management:

1. **Scope Planning** – Involves defining the project scope, verification, and control of the project scope, and how the WBS will be created. The scope management plan is created by the project team as the main output of the project scope planning process.

2. **Scope Definition** – This involves reviewing the project charter and all preliminary scope statements created during the project initiation stage, and adding more detailed information during the planning process as new requirements are developed and change requests are approved by either the project manager or by the CCB (Change Control Board). The main outputs of the scope definition are the, project scope statement, change request to the project, and all the updates to the project scope management plan.

3. **Creating the WBS** – This is the process of subdividing the major deliverables into smaller and smaller, more

manageable task. The main outputs are the WBS (work breakdown structure), dictionary, a project scope baseline, change request, updates to the project scope statement and project scope management plan.

4. **Scope Verification** – This involves customer acceptance of the project scope. The sponsor of the project, and in many instances, the stakeholders inspect and then formally verify and accept the deliverables of the project during this process. If for some reason the project deliverables are not acceptable, the sponsor will request changes, through a formal change request system, and the changes will be made to the product to meet the customer requirements.

5. **Scope Control** – This involves controlling all changes to the project scope. This processes involved in scope control are identifying, evaluating, and implementing changes to the project scope as the project progresses.

Scope Planning and Scope Management Plan

When performing scope planning, remember the main output is the scope management plan. The scope management plan is a formal document that includes descriptions of how the project team will prepare the project scope statement, create the WBS, verify completions of the project deliverables, and control change request to the project scope

Sample Project Charter

Project Title: XP Upgrade
Project Start Date: May 1, 2008
Projected Finish Date: October 29, 2008
Project Manager: Mike Williams, Ex: 2134,
mike.williams@website.com
Project Objectives: Upgrade the current Desktop and laptop environment, that is running on windows 2000, to Windows XP. These are the new Corporate standards as of March 30, 2008.
Budgeted: $2,600,000 for tech-refresh of existing hardware, and purchasing of new hardware.

Approach:

- Update the corporate database to reflect the new Windows licenses.
- Create a detailed project cost estimate for the XP Upgrade project for Sr. Management.
- Issue a request for quote from vendors to obtain best license cost.
- Use internal and consulting staff to perform the project.
- Setup staging area for Tech-Refresh and New desktops & Laptops.
- Setup distribution channels for shipping of hardware.
- Setup customer acceptance processes.

Sample Project Charter Continued:

Roles and Responsibilities:

Name	Role	Responsibility
Rick Marsh	CEO	Project Sponsor
Tom Rittenhouse	CIO	Monitor Project, Provide Staff
Mike Williams	PM	Plan, Execute, & Close Project
Bill Wilson	Director IT	Provide resources to PM
Sue Lindsey	Director Purchasing	Purchase Hardware & Licenses

Sign-Off:

Rick Marsh CEO	Tim Rittenhouse CIO
Mike Williams PM	Ed Wilson Director IT
John Lindsey DP	

Comments:

This project must be held to a strict timeline so that it does not interfere with the Christmas selling season.

Scope Definition

It is very important to have a good scope definition for the projects success. A good scope definition improves the accuracy of time, cost, and resource estimates, it defines a baseline for performance measurement and project control, and it assist in communicating clear work responsibilities. The main output of scope definition is a good project scope statement.

Project Scope Statement

The project scope statement is of great importance to a project. A project scope statement should include, at minimum, the following:

- A description of the project.
- Overall objectives and justifications.
- A detailed description of all the project deliverables.
- The characteristics and requirements of the product and or service to be produced.

An up-to-date project scope statement is an important document for maintaining and confirming a common understanding of the project scope.

Sample Project Scope Statement
Project Scope Statement

Servers: This project will need to purchase 200 new pSeries AIX Servers to support the new Central Data Center. The servers will be divided into three classes. 1.) for Database Servers, 2.) Web Servers, and 3.) Application Support Servers. The detailed layout of the servers will be in Appendix "B" along with the plans describing where they will be located.

NOTES:

Chapter 5

Project Integration Management

What is Project Integration Management?

Project integration management is the process of coordinating all the other project management knowledge areas into a cohesive project life cycle. Project integration management gives us the ability to bring all the elements of a project together at the right time to complete the project on time, in scope, and in budget.

The *PMBOK Guide 2004* names seven main processes involved in project integration management:

1. **Develop the project charter** – This is performed by working with the project stakeholders to create the project charter.

2. **Develop the preliminary project scope statement** – This serves as a high-level scope requirements document. You gain this document by working with the stakeholders and the end-users of the product or service being developed.

3. **Develop the project management plan** – This comes about by working with the sponsor and your project team to coordinate all team efforts to create a coherent, well thought-out document called the project management plan.

4. **Direct and manage project execution** – This is the job of the project manager. He or she is to carry out the project management plan by executing all the activities in the plan.

5. **Monitor and control the project work** – this is the process of overseeing all the project work being performed and making sure that all the project objective are being met by the team.

6. **Perform integrated change control** – You need to put a change control process in place so all changes

that effect the projects deliverables and organizational assets are followed to the letter.

7. **Close the project** – This is the final process used in managing a a project. This involves finalizing all project processes and activities so the team can formally close the project.

Work Breakdown Structure (WBS)

The work breakdown structure is used during the planning stage of the project. After completing the scope planning processes, the next step in project integration management, and also part of the scope management process, is developing the WBS. The WBS is a deliverable oriented grouping of the work to be performed on the project. A WBS is often laid out in a task-oriented family tree of activities, similar to a company's organizational chart. The project team normally builds the WBS around the projects product, project phase, or using the project management process groups. Most project teams like to build a WBS in chart form first. This gives the team the ability to visualize the whole project and all of its main parts or sections. In Figure 5.1A are examples of the WBS:

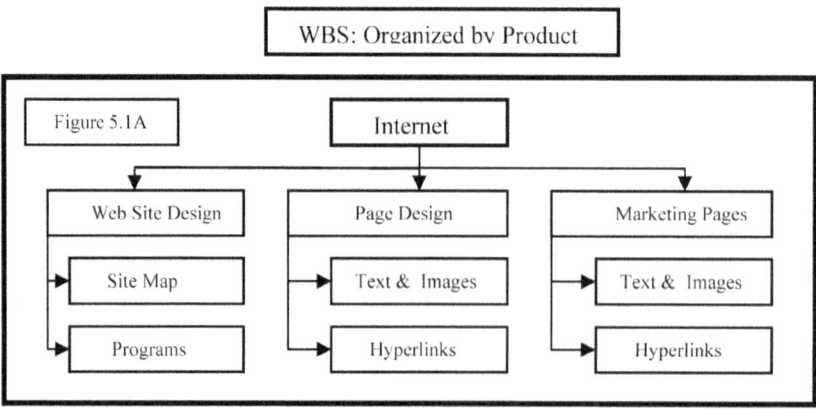

The WBS for Figure 5.1A is designed with the product areas providing the basis for its organizational layout.

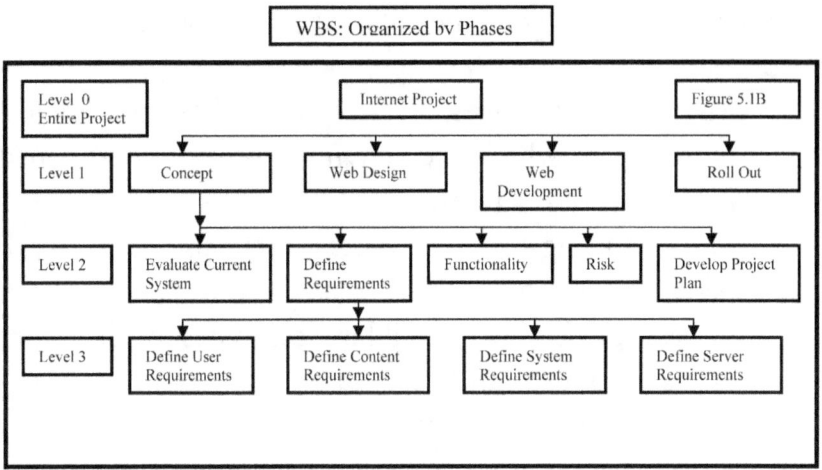

The WBS in Figure 5.1B is organized and designed around project Phases.

Using the WBS as a Validation Tool

At the higher levels the WBS is often broken down into phases or stages. These are often viewed as parts of work to be performed, delineated by deliverables, milestones, or management decisions that will authorize all the future work. In other words, the WBS summarizes all the subdivided work elements in the work plan.

The WBS is a functional decomposition diagram which is milestone driven until its very lowest level of work packages are reached. Thus, a top-down development approach yields progressively better defined work products.

A bottom-up approach, in many cases, used to develop estimates. In other words, planning is done from the highest or global level down to the work packages. Estimating is done using work packages as units of analysis that are then aggregated to form the project totals. When examining the WBS, at the lowest levels, is where the sub-activities and work packages emerge. The following is a list of the WBS purposes:

- The work packages is used to define the logical sequence in which the activities could be performed in a network diagram.
- The planning-team members then use each work package on a directional basis for estimating. Each discrete piece of work will have estimates for duration, assets, resources, and cost. The team should be asking the following questions?

1. How long will the work take to complete the project?
2. How many assets and resources will be used to complete the project?
3. To complete the project, what will the total cost be?

- By using work packages, the team will have the ability to capture the technical and performance objective for the project. Each work package must produce some kind of deliverable or product. Therefore, when you create a the WBS for a project, you automatically create an index of deliverables. This is a master list of documentation items that flow from each piece of work on the WBS. Each deliverable also has a quality standard associated with it.
- Another use for the WBS is to assign accountability and develop a responsibility assignment matrix for each work package and work product on the project. This a usually a spreadsheet where work packages are in a row or rows, and organizational units are the columns.

- The WBS is also used as a toll for risk analysis. During the planning process, the team builds the detailed WBS, and during this building of the WBS, risk can be identified, and risk analysis process can be used to mitigate these risk. This will, in turn, affect the estimating of the work, because team members must now factor in the probability of these occurrences and the likely impact they will have on the project.

- Remember that the WBS is a foundation for detailed planning, controlling work in progress, management reporting, change control, and project closure. Put this way, the WBS becomes the basis for tracking all work performed on the project, variance analysis, and corrective actions taken on the project. Figure 5.1A, and 5.1B gave examples of how to build a Work Breakdown Structure (WBS). You will need to apply these tools to perform the project task successfully, and complete the project on time, in scope, and within the allocated budget.

-

NOTES:

Chapter 6

Project Risk
Management

Basic Definition: Uncertainty

Risk is actually a measure of the amount of uncertainty that exists. It's directly related to information, as Figure 6.1 illustrates. This is not exactly the way most of us think of risk in your everyday life. However, in the world of Project Management, risk relates primarily to the extent of your ability to predict a particular outcome with at least a certain amount of correctness.

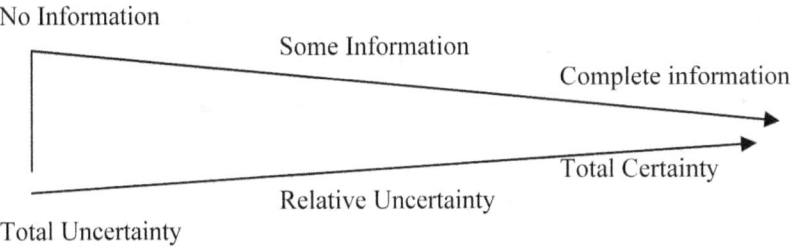

Figure 6.1

This interpretation is derived from the study if decision and risk analysis, the statistical sibling to project risk management.

Threat

The effects of risk can be positive or negative on a project. Positive effects of risk are often referred to as opportunities. Threats are the negative, or downside effects of risk, in risk management, and must be identified.

Definition of Risk Management Plan

It is the documentation of the procedures to be used to manage risk during the life of a project and the parties responsible for managing various areas of risk.

Risk Management

You need to remember that projects are investments and the project manager is the key person responsible for achieving these specific outcomes of the project within targets of time, cost, asset utilization, and resource utilization. Also, remember that every investment has inherent risk. I will address in this book the project risk and project contingencies next in this chapter.

Risk management occurs throughout the life of any and all projects, with increasing levels of detail at each phase or milestone of the project. Whenever it occurs, the essential elements of risk assessment are the following:

- **Risk management planning**
- **Risk identification**
- **Qualitative risk analysis**
- **Quantitative risk analysis**
- **Risk response planning**
- **Risk monitoring and control**

The first three elements listed can be summarized in a table that asks the project team to identify the risks and then categorize them in two dimensions: The likelihood of the risk occurring. The consequences and impact on the project. The results are then used to populate the cells in the table shown in Figure 6.2

		IMPACT		
		Low	Moderate	High
Probability	High			
	Moderate			
	Low			

After the risk have been identified and measured, the next stage in risk management are to develop the appropriate responses to the risk, and then monitor and control all risk that have been identified. These stages must deal with:

1. Prevention
2. Detection
3. Mitigation of damages and or loss.
4. Emergency procedures and responses.
5. A detailed damage assessment plan.
6. Restoration and damage recovery.

Project Contingency

A project contingency is used in a project when one or more conditions arises during the project that either effects the projects scope, schedule/time, budget, or the projects deliverable. A contingency plan must be worked out with the project sponsor in advance to address these problems when they come to light. The following contingency table can be used to address these problems (Figure 6.3)

Figure 6.3

CONTINGENCY TABLE

	PROBLEM		
	Low	Moderate	High
Problem Resolution One			
Two			
Three			

Once a problem has come to light the project manager and the project team must utilize the project contingency plans that have been worked out in advance, with the project sponsor.

NOTES:

Chapter 7

Project Time Management

What is Time Management?

Time management, when it pertains to a project, is the project schedule that was developed early on in the project. This schedule is used to keep the project deliverables on time during each phase of the project, and it involves the processes required to ensure timely completion of a project.

The importance of a Project Schedule

Many Information Technology Managers often cite delivering projects on time as one of the biggest problems or challenges. Managers also cite schedule issues as causing the most conflicts on projects during and throughout a project's timeline. Most of the schedule conflicts arise during the middle and end phases, schedule issues are the predominant source of conflict. If a project schedule is not adhered to during the duration of the project, the project will most likely fail.

Project Time Management Processes

There are six main processes used during project time management.

- **Activity definition** – This involves identifying the specific activities that the project team and stakeholders must perform to produce the project deliverables. An activity or task is an element of work normally found on the WBS that has an expected duration, a cost, and resource requirement.
- **Activity sequencing** - This involves identifying and documenting the relationships between project activities.
- **Activity resource estimating** – This involves estimating how many resources – people, equipment, and

materials a project team should use to perform all the project tasks.

- **Activity duration estimating** - This involves estimating the number of periods that are required to complete each individual task.
- **Schedule development** – This involves analyzing the task sequences, activity resource estimates, and activity duration estimates to create the project schedule.
- **Schedule control** – This involves controlling and managing changes to the project schedule.

Creating a Network Diagram

The best way to manage you time during a project is to use a "Network Diagram". When scheduling activities or task the process consists of identifying the specific activities that you'll be scheduling for completing the project. Once this has been completed you are in the position to create a "Network Diagram.

The network diagramming process begins by defining the relationship that will exist among task or activities. The most common graphical convention for drawing a network diagram is the Precedence Diagramming Method (PDM). The PDM diagram uses boxes that represent task or activities. The relationship between the task or activities is indicated with arrows. (Figure 7.1)

Figure 7.1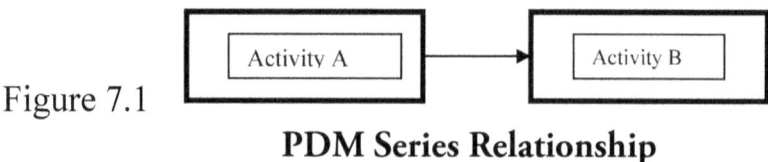

PDM Series Relationship

This other type of relation occurs when two task or activities can be done at the same time: a parallel relationship. (Figure 7.2)

Figure 7.2

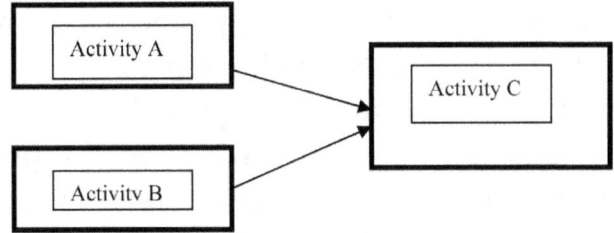

PDM Parallel Relationship

The parallel relationship is one way of showing a Network Diagram. In this Network Diagram example, activity "A" and activity "B" must both be finished before activity "C" can begin.   Note, in this example, that there is no relationship, or implied relationship between activities "A" and "B", as there's no arrow connecting the two. However, in some case, a relationship could exist between the two activities that could be completed in parallel. This type of relationship will link either the start or the finish of two activities. (Figure 7.3)

Figure 7.3

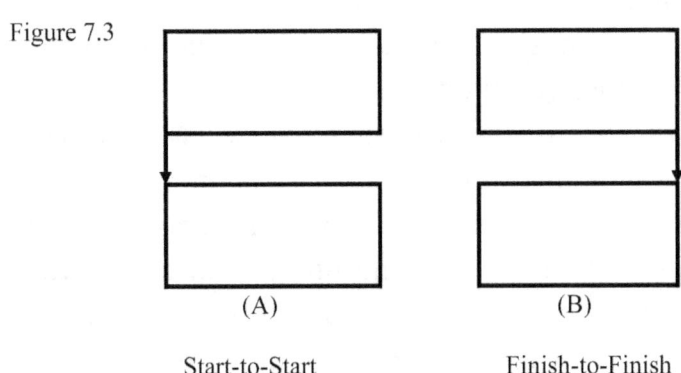

(A)	(B)
Start-to-Start	Finish-to-Finish

PDM Parallel Relationship

Figure 7.3 show and example of these kinds of relationships. A Start-to- Start relationship (A), and a Finish-to-Finish relationship (B).

Believe it or not, this is all you need to know to get started creating your own Network Diagram.

You start by reviewing your WBS, where you have identified the task or activities to schedule, track, and control. The process is quite simple. While you consider each individual task or activity, you will begin to consider the interrelationship that exist between those activities and others. For each task or activity, ask yourself the following questions:

- Think – What activities must be completed before this task or activity can start?
- What task or activities cannot start until this one is complete?
- What task or activities could be worked on at the same time as this task or activity?

Estimating Activity Durations

Now that you have modeled the logic with a network diagram, you be ready to move to the next step in scheduling. Estimating how long it will take to complete the project. There are two main methods:

The first is to characterize the length of a task or activity as effort. Effort is defined as the number of labor hours that task performers will be allowed to work on a given task or activity. A good way to look at it is, the billable time you will be charging on this project. The second way to characterize the length of a task or activity is duration. A good way to think of duration is a window of time within which the task or activity has to be competed. The key points to remember about the duration of a task or activity:

- Duration is the length of time that you would use for a task or activity when you place it on your project schedule.
- Duration is derived from considering the effort required to complete an appropriate adjustments for: The quantity of resources assigned to work on the task or activity.
  - The general availability of the resources.
  - Specific periods of inactivity or unavailability.
  - Weekends, and holidays.
  - Number of hours assumed in each work day and week.

Although duration appears to be a calculated quantity you should think of it as more of a negotiated figure and a kind of meeting of the minds than as a calculation.

Converting a Network Diagram to a Project Control Schedule

In the process briefly described above, steps 4-6 represent an iterative process that consists of combining the logical relationships you developed through network diagramming, your estimated activity duration, and any known constraints. The final result will be the project control schedule. The project control schedule is similar to a logic-based bar chart that has been "overlaid" on a calendar and approved by all parties involved in the project. It will provide the project manager, and the team, with all the information needed to monitor the project progress and maintain control over the project scheduled timelines. The following is and example of the "Project Control Schedule": Figure 7.4

Figure 7.4

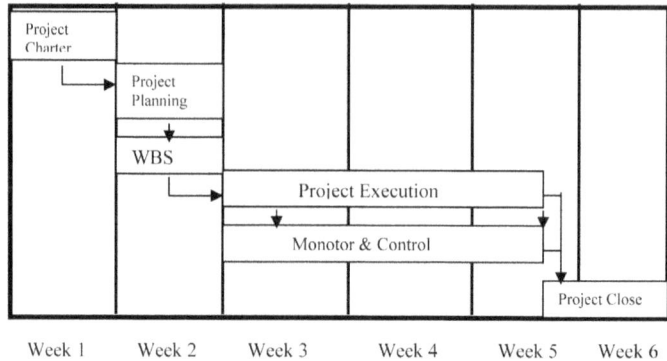

| Week 1 | Week 2 | Week 3 | Week 4 | Week 5 | Week 6 |

Calculating Critical Path

Now that you have prepared your schedule, you will begin to put in place a way to maintain project control and keep the project on schedule. Now we will address the critical path concept. In figure 7.4, do you notice that there is one set of activities that are continuously tied together with no breaks between them? This is the "Critical Path". Normally, an actual formula is used to determine the critical path, but now almost all project management software, like Microsoft Project 2003 has the ability built-in the software to perform the formula calculation for you. This being said, we will not be covering the critical path formula in this book.

In critical path analysis there are two performing manipulations of the schedule, "the forward pass, and the backward pass". The forward pass calculates the earliest time, and or dates, that the project task or activities can start and finish. The backward pass calculates the latest time, and or dates, that the project task or activities start and finish.

Gantt Charts

Gantt chats provide a workable standard format for which to display the project schedule information, by listing all the project activities and their corresponding start and finish dates in a workable calendar format. Many organization refer grant chart as bar charts since the task or activity start and end dates are represented as horizontal bars on the chart.

NOTES:

_____

_____

_____

_____

_____

_____

_____

_____

_____

_____

_____

_____

_____

_____

_____

_____

Chapter 8

Project Execution
& Closing

Project Execution

Project execution involves managing and performing the work laid out in the project management plan. In this chapter we will cover the steps to properly execute a project. Most of the project time is spent on execution of the project. During the project execution many different issues can come to light, and the project manager has be able to deal with these issue so as to be in a position to deliver the project on time, in scope, and in budget. Project integration management views project planning and execution as intertwined and inseparable activities. The main function of the creating a project management plan is to guide project execution though to completion.

Project Execution Tools and Techniques

Directing and managing project execution requires specialized tools and techniques, many of which are unique to project management.

- **Most Project Management Methodology** - experienced project managers believe that the most effective way to manage a project is to use some form of methodology that describes the how and what in managing a project.
- **Project management information system** – There are hundreds of different software packages on the market to help the project manager manage there projects. They range from powerful enterprise project management system that give you the ability to link the software to company portals so that the sponsor, and the project team can monitor the project progress, and individual project management packages that allow you work from you workstation anywhere you want.

Although these project management tools and techniques can assist in executing a project, the project manager must remember that positive leadership and strong teamwork are the core for running and completing any project successfully. Project managers and their teams are most often remembered by how well they delivered the project on time, in scope, and on budget.

Integrated Change Control

On most large projects, many project managers say that 80% to 90% of the job is communicating and managing changes to the project.

- **Integrated change control** – Primarily involves identifying, evaluating, and managing changes during the project life cycle. There are three main objectives of integrated change control:
1. Influencing the factors that cause the changes to ensure that the changes to the project are beneficial.
2. Determining that the change has actually occurred. The project manager has to know the status of the key project areas at all times during the life of the project. In addition, the project manager must communicate these changes to the sponsor and top management. You will find that the sponsor and top management do not like surprises during a project.
3. The project manager needs to manage the actual changes as they occur. Managing changes to the project is one of the key roles of the project manager and his team. It is important that a good change management system be put in place to minimizes changes to the project and prevent scope creep.

Change Control System

A change control system is a formal, documented process that describes how and when the official project documentation may be changed. The change control system also identifies the people with the authority to make changes to the project. A change control system often has a change control board (CCB), configuration management, and a process for communicating changes to the project.

- **Change Control Board** – Is a formal group of people that is responsible for approving and rejecting all changes to a project.
- **Configuration management** – Is to ensure that the descriptions of the project's product or service are correct and complete. It involves identifying and controlling the functional and physical design characteristics of the product or service and their support documentation.

Closing a Project

One of the most important steps in project management is the project closing process. This involves gaining the sponsor and stakeholders acceptance of the deliverables and bring the project or projects closing phase to and orderly end. This involves verifying that all of the project deliverable have been completed, and in many cases, includes a final sponsor presentation. It is very important to plan for and execute a smooth transition of the projects deliverable into the normal operations of the company. Table 7.5 provides a list of the knowledge areas, processes, and outputs of project closing based on the *"PMBOK·" Guide 2004.* Table 7.5:

Closing Processes and Output

Knowledge Area	Process	Outputs
Project Integration Management	Closing Project	* Administrative and Contract closure procedures * Final product, service, or result * organizational process assets (updates)
Project Procurement Management	Contract Closure	* Closed contracts * Organizational process assets (updates)

Now that the execution phase of a project has been complete and the team has moved into the closing process, during the closing process the project team should take the time to develop the appropriate closing procedures, deliver the final product or service of the project, and update any and all organizational process assets, such as the project files, and lessons-learned reports. If the project team has procured items, of any kind, during the project, they need to formally transition those item back to the company, and complete or close out all contracts. Table 7.6 provides the table of contents for the final project report. Table 7.6:

Final Project Report Table of Contents

1. Project Objectives
2. Summary of Project Results
3. Original and Actual Budgets
4. Original and Actual Start and End dates
5. Project a Success? What went right and what went wrong on the project?
6. Project Assessment – was the project completed on time, in scope and in budget, and was the deliverable acceptable to the sponsor and stakeholders?
7. Annual project benefits measurement approach
Attachments:
A. Project Management Documentation:
* Business Case
* Project Charter
* Team Contract
* Scope Statement
* WBS
* Baseline and Actual Gantt chart
* Milestone Report
* List of prioritized risks

* Contract files
* Lessons-learned reports and files
* Project Final presentation
* Client acceptance form and sign-off

B. Product Related Documentation:
* Survey and results
* Intranet site contents
*Intranet design documents
* Intranet site promotional information and documentation
* Intranet site roll-out information and documentation
* Summary of user request and inputs
* All test plans and reports
* project benefits measurement information and documentation

The project management process groups: initiating, planning, executing, monitoring and controlling and closing the project provides a useful framework for understanding and implementing the project management processes. These processes apply to most projects and, along with the project management knowledge areas.

NOTES:

Chapter 9

Project Methodologies

Project Life Cycle

All projects following some kind of life cycle. The project life cycle is the processes that are used to perform the project from beginning to end.

Systems Development Life Cycle

The system development life cycle (SDLC) is the framework for describing all the phases involved in developing information systems. Some of the most popular models of SDLS are the "Waterfall" model, the "Spiral model", the "incremental build model", the "prototyping model", and the "Rapid application development model" or RAD for short. These life cycle models are examples of a predictive life cycle, which means, that the scope of the project can be clearly articulated and the schedule and cost can be accurately predicted. On most projects the project team spends a lot of time on the project design and clarifying the project requirements. User are often unable to see tangible project results in the short term on project like software development. Below is a description of several predictive SDLC models.

Waterfall Life Cycle

The Waterfall life cycle model has well defined, linear stages or phases of systems development and support. This life cycle model assumes that requirements will remain stable after they are defined. The Waterfall life cycle model works in a proceeding order, which means that one phase of the project most be completed before the next phase can begin. Phase 1 must be completed before you can move on to phase 2 or phase 3.

Spiral Life Cycle

The spiral life cycle model was developed based on experience with various refinements of the waterfall model as applied to large government software projects. It recognizes the fact that most software developed using an iterative or spiral approach rather than a linear approach.

Incremental Build Life Cycle

The incremental build life cycle model provides for progressive development of operational software, with each release providing added software capabilities.

Prototyping Life Cycle

The prototyping life cycle model is used for developing software prototypes to clarify user requirements for operational software. It requires heavy user involvement, and developers use a model to generate functional requirements and physical design specifications simultaneously. Developers can throw out or keep the prototypes they have developed, but this usually depends on the software project.

Rapid Application Development Life Cycle

The rapid application development (RAD) life cycle model uses an approach in which developers work with an evolving prototype. This life cycle model also requires heavy user involvement and helps produce systems quickly without sacrificing the software's quality. Developers use RAD tools such as CASE (Computer aided software Engineering), JRP (Joint Requirements Planning), and JAD (Joint Application Design) to facilitate rapid prototyping and code generation on the project.

NOTES:

_____

_____

_____

_____

_____

_____

_____

_____

_____

_____

_____

_____

_____

_____

INDEX

www.ingramcontent.com/pod-product-compliance
Lightning Source LLC
Chambersburg PA
CBHW051548170526
45165CB00002B/931